THE SEVEN-LEAGUE CRUTCHES

Books by Randall Jarrell

THE SEVEN-LEAGUE CRUTCHES

LOSSES

BLOOD FOR A STRANGER

LITTLE FRIEND, LITTLE FRIEND

RANDALL JARRELL

The SEVEN-LEAGUE CRUTCHES

NEW YORK
HARCOURT, BRACE AND COMPANY

first edition

To

MACKIE

These poems have already been printed in *Poetry, The Kenyon Review, The Nation, Botteghe Oscure, The Virginia Quarterly Review, Partisan Review,* and *The Sewanee Review*. I'd like to thank these magazines for permission to reprint the poems; and to thank the John Simon Guggenheim Memorial Foundation for the opportunity to write several of them.

PRINTED IN THE UNITED STATES OF AMERICA

Contents

Europe

Children

Once upon a Time

EUROPE

The Orient Express

One looks from the train
Almost as one looked as a child. In the sunlight
What I see still seems to me plain,
I am safe; but at evening
As the lands darken, a questioning
Precariousness comes over everything.

Once after a day of rain
I lay longing to be cold; and after a while
I was cold again, and hunched shivering
Under the quilt's many colors, gray
With the dull ending of the winter day.
Outside me there were a few shapes
Of chairs and tables, things from a primer;
Outside the window
There were the chairs and tables of the world. . . .
I saw that the world
That had seemed to me the plain
Gray mask of all that was strange
Behind it—of all that *was*—was all.

But it is beyond belief.
One thinks, "Behind everything
An unforced joy, an unwilling

Sadness (a willing sadness, a forced joy)
Moves changelessly"; one looks from the train
And there is something, the same thing
Behind everything: all these little villages,
A passing woman, a field of grain,
The man who says good-bye to his wife—
A path through a wood all full of lives, and the train
Passing, after all unchangeable
And not now ever to stop, like a heart—

It is like any other work of art.
It is and never can be changed.
Behind everything there is always
The unknown unwanted life.

A Game at Salzburg

A little ragged girl, our ball-boy;
A partner—ex-Afrika-Korps—
In khaki shorts, P. W. illegible.
(He said: "To have been a prisoner of war
In Colorado iss a *privilege*.")
The evergreens, concessions, carrousels,
And D. P. camp of Franz Joseph Park;
A gray-green river, evergreen-dark hills.
Last, a long way off in the sky,
Snow-mountains.

Over this clouds come, a darkness falls.
Rain falls.
                    On the veranda Romana,
A girl of three,
Sits licking sherbet from a wooden spoon;
I am already through.
She says to me, softly: *Hier bin i'.*
I answer: *Da bist du.*

I bicycle home in my raincoat
Through the ponchos and pigtails of the streets,
Bathe, dress, go down four flights of stairs
Past Maria Theresa's sleigh
To the path to the garden, walk along the lake
And kick up, dreamily, the yellow leaves
Of the lindens; the pigeons are cooing
In the morning-glories of the gardener's house,
A dragonfly comes in from the lake.
The nymphs look down with the faces of Negroes,
Pocked, moled with moss;
The stone horse has sunk in marsh to his shoulders.

But the sun comes out, and the sky
Is for an instant the first rain-washed blue
Of becoming: and my look falls
Through falling leaves, through the statues'
Broken, encircling arms
To the lives of the withered grass,
To the drops the sun drinks up like dew.

In anguish, in expectant acceptance
The world whispers: *Hier bin i'.*

A Soul

It is evening. One bat dances
Alone, where there were swallows.
The waterlilies are shadowed
With cattails, the cattails with willows.

The moon sets; after a little
The reeds sigh from the shore.
Then silence. There is a whisper,
"Thou art here once more."

In the castle someone is singing.
"Thou art warm and dry as the sun."
You whisper, and laugh with joy.
"Yes, here is one,

"Here is the other . . . *Legs* . . .
And they move so?"
I stroke the scales of your breast, and answer:
"Yes, as you know."

But you murmur, "How many years
Thou hast wandered there above!
Many times I had thought thee lost
Forever, my poor love.

"How many years, how many years
Thou hast wandered in air, thin air!
Many times I had thought thee lost,
My poor soul, forever."

Hohensalzburg: Fantastic Variations on a Theme of Romantic Character

I should always have known; those who sang from the river,
Those who moved to me, trembling, from the wood
Were the others: when I crushed on a finger, with a finger,
A petal of the blossom of the lime, I understood
(As I tasted, under the taste of the flower, the dark
Taste of the leaf, the flesh that has never flowered)
All the words of the wood but a final word:
Pure, yearning, unappeasable—
A word that went on forever, like the roar
The peoples of the bees made in the limes.

When they called from the rushes I heard you answer:
I am a dweller of the Earth.

The old woman who sat beside her wheel
In her cottage under the hill, and gave you tea
When the mist crept up around her, evenings,
And you came to her, slowly, out of the mist
Where you had run, all evening, by the shore
Naked, searching for your dress upon the sand—
She would say to you, each evening: "What you do will do,
But not forever . . .
                    What you want is a husband and children."
And you would answer: *They will do,*
But not forever.
                    The old woman,
The stone maid sunk in the waters of the Earth
Who murmured, "You too are fair—
Not so fair as I, but fair as I was fair—"

These said to you, softly: "You are only a child.
What would you be, if you could have your wish?
You are fair, child, as a child is fair.
How would you look, if you could have your wish?"
You answered:
I would be invisible.

When I woke it was still night.
I saw, as I always saw,
A castle rising above limes—
A castle that has never been taken.
I felt in the map-pocket of the skirt
Of my leather coat, but mice had eaten the bar
Of chocolate, and left me foil like tinsel.
There was moonlight.
At the path out into the wood, a deer
Stood with stars in the branches of its antlers:
An iron deer.
Then there was nothing but night.
I felt at my hand
For an instant, the wing of a swallow—
Your hand opened across my hand.

I reached to you, but you whispered: *Only look.*
I whispered: "I see only moonlight."

I am here behind the moonlight.

You are there.
I thought at first
That you were only a ghost,
A ghost asleep in a castle that is asleep.
But these German ghosts—harsh clumsy things—
Haunt no one, but only change

Men into things, things into things.
Many a chandelier
Clouded with china roses, many a swan
Floating beside its shepherd, among cresses,
Many a star
Set in the antlers of an iron deer
Was once a sleeper wandering through the wood.
Some walked through the pits of the glade to a ghost
And were changed: a ghost wants blood;
And it will do—
but not forever.
But I shall be with you here forever:
Past the dust of thorns, past the sleepers wound
Like worms in the terrible chains of their breath,
I shall lie in your arms forever.
If you sleep I shall sleep, if you wake I shall wake,
If you die I shall also die.

You said: *I am then not dead?*

You are only sleeping . . .
When I come to you, sprawled there asleep
At the center of all the webs, at the final
Point of the world: one drop of your blood,
I shall bend to you, slowly—
You are asleep.
The leaves breathe with your breath. The last, least stir
Of the air that stumbles through a fur of leaves
Says the sound of your name, over and over, over and over;
But someday—
Years off, many and many years—
I shall come to you there asleep,
I shall take you and . . .
Tell me.

No, no, I shall never.
Tell me.
You must not know.
Tell me.
I—I shall kiss your throat.

My *throat?*

There, it is only a dream.
I shall not so—I shall never so.

I saw, in your eyes beside my eyes,
A gaze pure, yearning, unappeasable:
Your lips trembled, set
For an instant in the slightest smile
I ever saw;
Your cold flesh, faint with starlight,
Wetted a little with the dew,
Had, to my tongue, the bloom of fruit—
Of the flower: the lime-tree-flower.
And under the taste of the flower
There was the taste of—

I felt in the middle of the circle
Of your mouth against my flesh
Something hard, scraping gently, over and over
Against the skin of my throat.
I woke and fell asleep and woke:
Your face above me
Glowed faintly now—something light, a life
Pulsed there. When I saw that it was my blood,
I used my last strength and, slowly,
Slowly, opened my eyes
And pushed my arms out, that the moonlight pierced and held—

I said: "I want you"; and the words were so heavy
That they hung like darkness over the world,
And you said to me, softly: *You must not so.*
I am only a girl.
Before I was a ghost I was only a girl.

I said to you, "Before I was a ghost
I was only a—
a ghost wants blood:
When they find me, here except for my blood,
They will search for you all night—harsh clumsy things
In their tunics and leather shorts and pigtails.
All the badges along the bands of their hats will shine. . . .
When all but one has said to you, *Gute Nacht,*
And you have answered, are almost free
To call to me there in the bonds of the moonlight,
The last will mutter cunningly, *Grüss Gott.*
Then as all my blood
Flows from your limbs into your heart—
When, at the name of God,
You can say nothing, O dweller of the Earth—
You will cry out bitterly, and they will seize you
And bind you and boil you to death—the dead also die—
There at the fountain of the square
Just under the castle, by the iron deer;
Make of you a black-pudding, deck it with schillings and thaler,
And serve it, all *herrlich,* to the Man of the castle
With a sign stuck on it:
To eat is *verboten.*"

Or so it went once: I have forgotten. . . .

What shall I call you, O Being of the Earth?
What I wish you to call me I shall never hear.

We shall change; we shall change; but at last, their stars,
We shall rest in the branches of the antlers
Of the iron deer.
                    But not forever:
Many a star
Has fallen, many a ghost
Has met, at the path to the wood, a ghost
That has changed at last, in love, to a ghost—

We should always have known. In this wood, on this Earth
Graves open, the dead are wandering:
In the end we wake from everything.

Except one word—

In the end one wakes from everything.

                    Except one word
Goes on, always, under the years,
A word we have never understood—
And our life, our death, and what came past our life
Are lost within that steady sound:
Pure, yearning, unappeasable,
The one spell turns above us like the stars.

And yet surely, at the last, all these are one,
We also are forever one:
A dweller of the Earth, invisible.

An English Garden in Austria

(seen after *Der Rosenkavalier*)

It is as one imagined it: an English garden . . .

Mein Gott!—as all the little girls here say—
To see here the path, the first step of that first path
Our own great parents took! Today, *le Roi Soleil* shines
On his mistress's nuns' orphans' *Athalie;*
Saint-Simon, Leibnitz, and some wandering stars
Murmuring for joy together . . . and in the night
A Ruin, a Prospect, and one blasted tree
Lour on their progress; and next day where are they?

On such a path as this, a "rustic beau
[Or bear; one's doubtful, with this orchestration]
Of thirty-five" pauses to hear a man
Reciting in a big fur hat, with feeling—
And growls politely, "Metastasio?"
They whisper: "Quiet! That's J. J. Rousseau,"
And bear him off to the measures of a *Ländler*.
Helped to his coach, the Baron exits grumbling
About the "luck of all us Lerchenaus."

. . . It was not thus that you sang, Farinelli!
By graver stages, up a sterner way,
You won to those fields the candelabra lit,
Paused there; sang, as no man since has sung—
A present and apparent deity—the pure
Impossible airs of Arcady: and the calm
Horsehair-wigged shepherds, Gods of that Arcadian
Academy, wept inextinguishable tears.

Such power has music; and the repeated spell
Once a day, at evening, opened the dull heart
Of old mad Philip: all his courtiers wept
And the king asked, weeping: "Why have I wept?"
And Farinelli sang on; Ferdinand
Buried his father, ruled—
                                        and heard, paused, heard again:
The years went on, men withered, Farinelli sang.

You are silent now: you, Faustina Hasse,
Her husband Johann Adolf, the Abate
Metastasio . . . very silent.
They float past; seem to whisper, to the oat
Of a shepherd wintering very far from Weimar:
"We also have dwelt in Arcady."
                                                  —So Death.

The shades of your Grotto have encompassed me.
How can I make out, among these ruins, your Ruin?
You went for this pleasing terror to the past
And built it here, an image of the Possible:
Well ruined, Ruin! . . .
                                        But I come late.

In those years Europe lived beneath the lightning
Of the smile of that certain, all too certain spirit
Whom Almighty God—
                                        whom *le bon Dieu* sent for a rod
To these Philistines; he held out sixty years,
Gentling savage Europe with his Alexandrines,
Submitted, went up to Switzerland, and perished.
One spends one's life with fools, and dies among watches.
But see him in flower, in a Prussian garden.
He walks all summer, yawning, in the shade

Of an avenue of grenadiers; and a Great Person
In a tie-wig walks with this monkey, tags his verses,
And—glancing sideways, with suspicion—speaks of *Götz
Von Berlichingen mit der eisernen Hand.*
Said Frederick: "Here's the hand, but where's the glove?"
Or words to that effect; and next year jailed him
For having gone off with his (Pharaoh's) flute
In a sack of corn upon a baggage-camel.
Or words to that effect . . . Then all the world
Shifts to another gear: Count Almaviva and his valet
Shake hands, cry *Citoyen!* are coffined by a sad
Danton; assisting, Anacharsis Clootz—
To the Masons' Funeral Music of their maker.
And one might have seen, presiding among drummers,
An actress named *Raison* (*née* Diderot).
Meanwhile Susanna and the Countess sigh
For someone not yet on the scene; their man of tears
Retires, is rouged as Destiny: Rousseau
Comes in as Cain, upon a charger . . . Instead of his baton
This corporal carries *Werther* in his knapsack.
He reads it seven times, and finds no fault
Except with Werther: he was too ambitious.
The soldier nods—these buzzing Mamelukes
Have made him drowsy; shadows darken all the East
And over his feeling shoulder, as he sleeps,
Die Weltgeschichte peeps down upon his Sorrows.
(He wakes, smiles sleepily, and tweaks its ear.)
At Jena he shows his gratitude, says: "Here's a man!"
(What were the others? . . .
Dead men. He'd killed them every one.)
A vulgar demon, but our own: he still prepares us
"Plays worthy of the savages of Canada"—
Up from the floorboards soars the infernal
Everything that is deserves to perish,

And actors, author, audience die applauding.
Then he whispers, winking: "Politics is Destiny!"
And some *Spiessbürger,* some *aquarelliste,*
Some *Spielverderber* from a Georgian seminary
Echo him—higher, higher: *"Es muss sein!"*

"Others have understood the world; we change it."
"Truth is what works." "I have seen the Future and it works."

No Lerchenau was e'er a spoilsport,
A ghost sings; and the ghosts sing wonderingly:
Ist halt vorbei! . . . Ist halt vorbei! . . .

Then there is silence; a soft floating sigh.
Heut' oder morgen kommt der Tag,
And how shall we bear it?
                                        Lightly, lightly.

The stars go down into the West; a ghostly air
Troubles the dead city of the earth.

. . . It is as one imagined it: an English garden.

The Face

Die alte Frau, die alte Marschallin!

Not good any more, not beautiful—
Not even young.
This isn't mine.
Where is the old one, the old ones?
Those were mine.

It's so: I have pictures,
Not such old ones; people behaved
Differently then . . . When they meet me they say:
You haven't changed.
I want to say: You haven't looked.

This is what happens to everyone.
At first you get bigger, you know more,
Then something goes wrong.
You are, and you say: I am—
And you were . . . I've been too long.

I know, there's no saying no,
But just the same you say it. No.
I'll point to myself and say: I'm not like this.
I'm the same as always inside.
—And even that's not so.

I thought: If nothing happens . . .
And nothing happened.
Here I am.
                    But it's not *right.*
If just living can do this,
Living is more dangerous than anything:

It is terrible to be alive.

The Knight, Death, and the Devil

Cowhorn-crowned, shockheaded, cornshuck-bearded,
Death is a scarecrow—his death's-head a teetotum
That tilts up toward man confidentially
But trimmed with adders; ringlet-maned, rope-bridled,
The mare he rides crops herbs beside a skull.
He holds up, warning, the crossed cones of time:
Here, narrowing into now, the Past and Future
Are quicksand.
A hoofed pikeman trots behind.
His pike's claw-hammer mocks—in duplicate, inverted—
The pocked, ribbed, soaring crescent of his horn.
A scapegoat aged into a steer; boar-snouted;
His great limp ears stuck sidelong out in air;
A dewlap bunched at his breast; a ram's-horn wound
Beneath each ear; a spur licked up and out
From the hide of his forehead; bat-winged, but in bone;
His eye a ring inside a ring inside a ring
That leers up, joyless, vile, in meek obscenity—
This is the devil. Flesh to flesh, he bleats
The herd back to the pit of being.

In fluted mail; upon his lance the bush
Of that old fox; a sheep-dog bounding at his stirrup,
In its eyes the cast of faithfulness (our help,
Our foolish help); his dun war-horse pacing
Beneath in strength, in ceremonious magnificence;
His castle—some man's castle—set on every crag:
So, companioned so, the knight moves through this world.
The fiend moos in amity, Death mouths, reminding:
He listens in assurance, has no glance

To spare for them, but looks past steadily
At—at—
            a man's look completes itself.

The death of his own flesh, set up outside him;
The flesh of his own soul, set up outside him—
Death and the devil, what are these to him?
His being accuses him—and yet his face is firm
In resolution, in absolute persistence;
The folds of smiling do for steadiness;
The face is its own fate—*a man does what he must*—
And the body underneath it says: *I am.*

Nollekens

(In England during the last part of the eighteenth century there lived a very small, very childish man—a bad speller and a worse miser—who was the most famous portrait sculptor of his day. He had a dog called Cerberus, a cat called Jenny Dawdle, servants called Bronze and Mary Fairy, and a wife named Mary Welch. All that my poem says that he did, he did; I read about it in *Nollekens and His Times,* the book "the little Smith" wrote after Nollekens had died.)

Old Nollekens? No, Little Nollekens:
The Sculptor-Man. "Stand here and you will see
Nine streets commence," he told the little Smith,
Who counted them; "my mother showed them me."
He pricked the King's nose with the calipers.

He stood on King Street in his blue striped hose
And an old bag-wig—the true Garrick-cut—
And stated, in the voice of Samuel Johnson:
"Well, Mrs. Rapsworth, you have just done right.
I wore a pudding as a little boy;
My mother's children all wore puddings."
But Johnson said to him, once: "Bow-wow-wow!"

Dog-Jennings, Shakespeare Steevens, the Athenian
Stuart—these, these too, recalled with joy
The unique power of a Mr. Rich
Who scratched his ear with one foot, like a dog.
It took as much wit as the *are-bolloon.*

The milk-maids danced on May-day, and were paid;
The butchers' snow-house was signed: *Nollekens;*
He stole the nutmegs from the R. A.'s punch—
And once gave Cerberus but half his paunch

And told him, "You have had a roll today."
But Mary Fairy scolded Nollekens,
And old Bronze put her arm around his neck
And asked him how he did. Said Nollekens,
"What! now you want some money—I've got none.
Can you dance?" "Dance, Sir! why, to be sure I can.
Give me the cat." While he watched Jenny Dawdle,
His tabby, dancing round the room with Bronze,
The tears of pleasure trickled down his cheeks
Upon his bib.
                    And yet one day he fell
Into a passion with this favorite cat
For biting the old feather of a pen
He kept to oil the hinges of the gate.
(He showed it to her, and explained to her
The mischief she had done.) So, catching rats,
He stuffed the rat-trap with a pound of cheese
To catch them all at once; so, from the Tower
He went to model George, and cried: "They've got
Such lions there! The biggest did roar so;
My heart, he did roar so." The Sculptor roared.

In winter, when the birds fell from the branches,
In winter, when his servant fed the beggars,
His wife called, "Betty! Betty! Give them this.
Here is a bone with little or no meat upon it."
One, looking at the other steadfastly,
Repeated: "Bill, we are to have a bone
With little or no meat upon it."
                                        So.

He left two hundred thousand pounds—and two
Old shoes, the less worn of his last two pairs;

One night-cap, two shirts, and three pairs of stockings;
And the coat in which he married Mary Welch.

Was "Mrs. White delivered of a sun"?
Who measured the dead Pitt? Ah, Nollekens,
To smuggle lace in busts! To leave poor Bronze
But twenty pounds! And yet, whoever dies?

"Ring a bell, ring a bell, my pretty little maid?—
Why, that I will." And I see straining for it
The crescent, tiptoe Nollekens. . . . "My heart,
To sit there in the dark, to save a candle—"
I grieve; but he says, looking steadfastly,
"If you laugh, I'll make a fool of ye."
And I nod, and think acquiescingly:
"Why, it is Nollekens the Sculptor."

The Truth

When I was four my father went to Scotland.
They *said* he went to Scotland.

When I woke up I think I thought that I was dreaming—
I was so little then that I thought dreams
Are in the room with you, like the cinema.
That's why you don't dream when it's still light—
They pull the shades down when it is, so you can sleep.
I thought that then, but that's not right.
Really it's in your head.

And it was light then—light at *night.*
I heard Stalky bark outside.
But really it was Mother crying—
She coughed so hard she cried.
She kept shaking Sister,
She shook her and shook her.
I thought Sister had had her nightmare.
But he wasn't barking, he had died.
There was dirt all over Sister.
It was all streaks, like mud. I cried.
She didn't, but she was older.
                                        I thought she didn't
Because she was older, I thought Stalky had just gone.
I got *everything* wrong.
I didn't get one single thing right.
It seems to me that I'd have thought
It didn't happen, like a dream,
Except that it was light. At night.
They burnt our house down, they burnt down London.
Next day my mother cried all day, and after that

She said to me when she would come to see me:
"Your father has gone away to Scotland.
He will be back after the war."

The war then was different from the war now.
The war now is *nothing*.

I used to live in London till they burnt it.
What was it like? It was just like here.
No, that's the truth.
My mother would come here, some, but she would cry.
She said to Miss Elise, "He's not himself";
She said, "Don't you love me any more at all?"
I was *my*self.
Finally she wouldn't come at all.
She never said one thing my father said, or Sister.
Sometimes she did,
Sometimes she was the same, but that was when I dreamed it.
I could tell I was dreaming, she was just the same.

That Christmas she bought me a toy dog.

I asked her what was its name, and when she didn't know
I asked her over, and when she didn't know
I said, "You're not my mother, you're not my mother.
She *hasn't* gone to Scotland, she is dead!"
And she said, "Yes, he's dead, he's dead!"
And cried and cried; she *was* my mother,
She put her arms around me and we cried.

The Contrary Poet

(Tristan Corbière)

On the coast of ARMORICA. A monastery.
The winds complained, inside: *Another windmill;*
    All the donkeys of the county
Came to grate their teeth off in the seedy ivy
Of a wall so holey that no living man
    Had ever come in through the doorway.

Alone—but still on its own feet, full of poise,
Corrugated as the jaw of an old woman,
Its roof knocked onto the corner of its ear,
Gaping like a ninny, the tower stood there

As vain as ever: it had its memories. . . .
It wasn't anything but a nest of black sheep,
Lovers from the bush, a rat down on his luck,
Stray dogs, benighted hobos—smugglers and customs-inspectors.

One year, the tenant of this low tower
Was a wild poet with a ball in his wing
Fallen among owls: the venerable owls
Who, from some height, considered him.—He respected their
    holes—
He, the only paying owl, as his lease stated:
Twenty-five écus a year: door to be replaced.

As for the people of the place, he didn't see them:
Only, passing by, they looked from below,
    Turning their noses up at his window;
The priest guessed that he was a leper;

And the mayor answered: "What can *I* do?
He's more likely an Englishman . . . some such creature."

The women learned—no doubt from the buzzards—
That he *lived in concubinage with the Muses!* . . .
In short, a heretic . . . Some Parisian
From Paris or some such place?—Alas, nobody knew a thing.
He was invisible; and as *his Wenches*
Didn't advertise themselves, nobody said a word.

As for him, he was simply an idler, tall, thin, pale;
An amateur hermit, chased in by a squall. . . .
The far green fields—the feverish ones—he'd loved too well.
Given up by process-servers, by physicians,
He had lit here, fed up, looking for a spot
To die by himself or to live by default. . . .

Making, from something almost like an artist,
Something almost like a philosopher;
Rain or shine, always complaining;
Off any human track.

There remained to him a hammock, a hurdy-gurdy,
A spaniel who slept under the name of Fido.
No less faithful, sad and sweet as she,
Was another companion: he called it Ennui.

Dying in his sleep, he lived in dreams.
His dreams were the tide that rose on the shore,
The tide that fell.
Sometimes, vaguely, he took up waiting. . . .
Waiting for what . . . the tide to rise—the tide to fall—
Someone . . . Who knows?

He knows! . . . Floating in the wind of his watch-tower,
Has he forgotten how quick are the dead?
He? Which *he?* the stray ghost? the dilapidated
Body searching for its own ill-buried spirit?

Surely, She isn't far—She for whom you bellow,
O Stag of St. Hubert! Ah, sad flameless forehead. . . .
Poor old sport, have they dug you up without a permit?
Play dead if you can . . . For She has wept for you!

—But could he, He? Wasn't he a poet . . .
Immortal as any other? . . . And inside his poor head,
His moved-out-of head, he still could feel them,
The hexameters marching their catercornered rounds.

For want of knowing how to live, he kept alive—
For want of knowing how to die, he wrote:

"Dear, this is someone dead for so many ages
In that poet's heart of yours, he's already a myth.
I rhyme, therefore I am . . . but don't be afraid, it's *blank*
—The shell of an oyster torn from its bed!
I've pinched myself all over: it's me. Last mistake
En route to Heaven—for my niche is high as that!—
I asked myself, all ready to take wing:
Heads or tails . . . —And here I am, still asking. . . .

"It was to you I said, *Good-bye to life.*
How you wept! I watched you crying for me
Till it made me want to stay and help you cry.
But it's over now: I'm just a doting ghost,
Some bones and (I was going to say *flesh*). There's no mistake.
It's me all right, here I am—but like an erasure.

"We were connoisseurs of all the curiosities:
Notice this *objet d'art.*—I'm sick of it.—
In my distastes especially, I had good taste.
You know, I have let go of Life with gloves.
The Other one wouldn't touch with tweezers. . . .
I'm looking for *something different* for this—window-dummy.

"Come back to me: Your eyes in these eyes here! Your lips
Upon these lips! . . . Feel how hot my face is—here: that's You,
It's You I'm sick with . . . Remember?—those nights that could
        have burned
The rainbow out of heaven—
                                        what's become of it? It's charcoal.
And that star? . . . It's no use looking for the star
    You tried to see upon my brow.
    A spider has set its web
    At the same spot—on the ceiling.

"I am a stranger.—Perhaps it's better so.
Isn't it? . . . No, come back and notice me a little.
You always doubted, Thomas: I want to see your faith,
I want to see you touch the wound and whisper:—You!—

"Come finish me off again—it's quite amusing:
You'll see my harvests from your bedroom . . . it's December;
My great fir-forests, the golden flowers of broom,
My heather of Armorica . . . piled on the andirons.
Come gorge yourself on fresh air. Here there's a breeze
So crisp! . . . the ends of my roof curl.
The sun's so mild . . . it freezes all the time.
The spring . . . —Spring, isn't it your twenty years?
It's you I'm waiting for: look, already a swallow
. . . Nailed to my turret, a rusty swallow.
Soon we can go gathering mushrooms. . . .

On my staircase, gilded . . . by a candle-end.
On the greening wall a dried-up periwinkle
Exists. . . . Then we'll take the waters, lie there drying
On the sand-dunes with the other driftwood.
The sea coos its *Lullaby for Castaways;*
A barcarole at dusk . . . for the wild ducks.

"Like *Paul* and *Virginia*—virginal, if you wish—
We'll graze on the grass of our lost paradise. . . .
Or *Robinson* with *Friday*—why, it's easy:
The rain has made an island of my kingdom.

"But if, near me, you're afraid of being lonely,
We've friends, plain honest ones—a poacher;
Not to count that blue cloak that habitually
Paces its rounds and holds a customs-inspector. . . .
No more process-servers! I've got moonlight,
I've got friends—all poor broke lovesick fools.

—"And our nights! *Whispering I know not what of wild and sweet,*
Nights for a Romeo!—Day will never break.—
Aurora awak'ning, burst from the bonds of sleep,
Dropping her white sheet . . . stops up my chimney.
Look, my nightingales! . . . nightingales of the tornado,
Gay as larks, wailing like screech-owls!
My weathercock, way up there, rubs the rust off his yodel,
And you can hear my Aeolian door lamenting
As did Saint Anthony in his temptation . . .
Come, pretty limb of Sata—of seduction!

"Hoy! the rats in the garret are dancing farandoles!
The roof's slates rattle down like castanets!
The witches in my belfry—
No, I've not one witch!

"Ah, but wouldn't I retail my skin to Satan
If he'd only tempt me with a little ghost—
You. I see you everywhere, but white as a seer
I worship you . . . And that's pitiful: to worship what one loves!
Appear, a dagger in thy heart!—That's it,
You know, like *Inès de La Sierra*. . . .
A knock . . . Someone's there! . . .
Alas! it's a rat.

"I daydream . . . and it's always you. On everything
Your memory perches, like a mocking spirit:
My loneliness . . . —*You!*—My owls with golden eyes:
—*You!*—My crazy weathercock: oh, *You!*—Any more?—
—*You!* my shutters flinging their arms out to the storm. . . .
A far-off voice: Your song!—this is ecstasy!
The squalls that beat at Your lost name—this is crazy . . .
Crazy, but it's You! My heart, wide open
As my own disordered shutters,
Beats in senseless circles, to the breath
Of the most fantastic gusts.

"Wait . . . a ready shadow, for an instant, came
To trace your profile on the naked wall,
And I turned my head—to hope or to remember—
Sister Anne, Sister Anne, do you see no one coming?

"No one . . . I see—I see, in my cold chamber,
My bed padded with its push-cart satin
And my dog asleep on it—poor beast—
And I laugh . . . because it makes me a little sick.

"I've used, to summon you, my hurdy-gurdy and my lyre;
My heart's cracked jokes—the imbecile—to fool itself. . . .
Come weep, if my lines have made you laugh;
Come laugh, if they have made you weep. . . .

"It will be comical. . . . Come play at poverty.
Back to Nature: *Come live with me and be my love. . . .*
It's raining in my hearth, it's raining in my heart:
In my late heart.
                    Come! my candle's out, I've no more fire."

* * *

His lamp went out. He opened the window.
The sun was rising. He looked at his letter,
Laughed and tore it up . . . The little white pieces
Seemed, through the fog, a flight of gulls.

A Rhapsody on Irish Themes

At six in the morning you scratched at my porthole,
Great-grandmother, and looked into my eyes with the eyes
Of a potato, and held out to me—only a dollar—
A handkerchief manufactured with their own hands
By the Little People; a *Post* wet from no earthly press,
Dreamed over the sinking fire
                                        of a pub by a Papal Count.
Look: a kerchief of linen, embroidered cunningly
In the green of Their hearts, in Their own hand:
A SOUVENIR OF OLD IRELAND.

Then you turned into the greatest of the gulls
That brood on the seesaw green
Swells of the nest of the harbor of Cóbh.

All is green, all is small, all is—
It is nôt; the nuns sailing to Ireland
Disembark, and are dovetailed into the black
Nuns sailing from Ireland: a steady state,
But black. And that patch of the red of blood
On the hillside without any trees, by the topless
Tower, is a Cardinal surely? the steak
This Lady with Cromwell's sword in her suitcase
Wolfs for her lonely supper, with a sigh
Like an empire falling? And the sky is the blue
Of the fat priest's brimmed beret,
Of the figuring and clasps of his new
Accordion (that plays all night, by itself, like the sword
Of a hero, a *Mother Machree*
That'd tear your heart out entirely).

The soft, guileful, incessant speech
Plaits into the smack of the feet
In their dance on the deck, every night in the moonlight;
The smile is, almost, the smile
Of the nuns looking on in delight—
The delight of a schoolgirl at recess, a trouble to no one.
But—blue eyes, gray face—
I was troubled by you.

The old woman, met in sleep,
Skinned herself of her wrinkles, smiled like a goddess—
Skinned herself of the smile, and said to me softly:
"There's no rest for you, grandson, till you've reached the land
Where, walking the roads with an adding-machine on your
shoulder,
You meet no one who knows it."
Well, I hold nothing
Against you but what you are. One can almost bear
The truth in that soft shameless speech
That everything is a joke—from your Sublime
To your Ridiculous is one false step
(And, as you say, the *Herr Geheimrat*
Is the cut of a cast of Apollo; *Monseigneur*
An *émigré* from a death in Saint-Simon
And Bishop in Maryland—Baltimore, Maryland:
What counts is Religion
and Politics.
I know, I know—they all say so at home;
But at home they mean money—do you mean money?);
But one settles at birth on that step of the stair
And dislikes being shown that there's nothing there.
But I believe you: the orchestration
Of this world of man is all top or bottom,

And the rest is—
anything that you say.
To argue longer would be un-Irish,
Unnatural grandson that I am!

—Great-grandson.

Old sow, old Circe, *I'm* not your farrow.
Yet ah, to be eaten! There honk beside me the Tame Geese
Of the Seven Hills of the City of Dublin,
And it's Stentor I cough like, what with the smoke of peat—
Man is born to Ireland as the sparks fly upward:
A sleepwalker fallen from the edge of Europe,
A goosegirl great among publicans and censors.

—She speaks, smiling, of someone "who felt at home
In whatever was least like home, and fell in love
With the world for not being America"—
Old Sibyl!
It's your last leaf . . . Still, play it: it is so;
I'm from nowhere, I'm Nobody. But if I'm to be reminded
By any nobody—
Ireland, I've seen your cheeks
The red of dawn:
the capillaries are broken.

Long ago, the sun set. These are the Western Isles.

—And, waking, I saw on the Irish Sea
Orion, his girdle a cinch, and himself a hunter,
An Irish hunter . . .
that is to say, a horse.

Great-grandmother, I've dreamed of you till I'm hoarse.
It was all a lie: I take back every word.
. . . If your shin *is* speckled,

Your grin, alas! pious—
still, what a brow-ridge!
You Eden of Paleolithic survivals,
You enclave of Brünn and of Borreby man,
Fold your child home, when—weary of Learning—
He sighs for the Night of the Spirit of Man.

. . . What have I said! Faith, I'm raving entirely:
Your taste is like lotus, you Irish air!
Get the wax out of your ears, you oarsmen,
We sail at six . . . And here's the last lesson
I learned from you, Ireland:

what it is I've forgotten.

Well, what if it's gone? Here're some verses of Goethe's—
An old upright man, a lover of Ireland—
You Senate of Ireland, to straighten the conduct
Of such of your people as need it: *In peace*
Keep tidy
Your little coops.
In war
Get along
With quartered troops.

The Olive Garden

(Rainer Maria Rilke)

He went up under the gray leaves
All gray and lost in the olive lands
And laid his forehead, gray with dust,
Deep in the dustiness of his hot hands.

After everything this. And this was the end.
—Now I must go, as I am going blind,
And why is it Thy will that I must say
Thou art, when I myself no more can find thee.

I find Thee no more. Not in me, no.
Not in others. Not in this stone.
I find Thee no more. I am alone.

I am alone with all men's sorrow—
All that, through Thee, I thought to lighten,
Thou who art not. O nameless shame . . .

Men said, later: an angel came.

Why an angel? Alas, there came the night
And leafed through the trees, indifferently.
The disciples moved a little in their dreams.
Why an angel? Alas, there came the night.

The night that came was no uncommon night;
So hundreds of nights go by.
There dogs sleep; there stones lie.
Alas a sorrowful, alas any night
That waits till once more it is morning.

For men beseech: the angels do not come,
Never do nights grow great around them.
Who lose themselves, all things let go;
They are renounced by their own fathers
And shut from their own mothers' hearts.

A Conversation with the Devil

Indulgent, or candid, or uncommon reader
—I've some: a wife, a nun, a ghost or two—
If I write for anyone, I wrote for you;
So whisper, when I die, *We was too few;*
Write over me (if you can write; I hardly knew)
That I—that I—but anything will do,
I'm satisfied. . . . And yet—
                                        and yet, you *were* too few:
Should I perhaps have written for your brothers,
Those artful, common, unindulgent others?

Mortal men, man! mortal men! So says my heart
Or else my belly—some poor empty part.
It warms in me, a dog beside a stove,
And whines, or growls, with a black lolling smile:
I never met the man I didn't love.
Life's hard for them . . . these mortals . . . Lie, man, lie!
Come, give it up—this whining poetry;
To any man be anything. If nothing works,
Why then, Have Faith.
                                        That blessed word, Democracy!

But this is strange of you: to tempt me now!
It brings back all the past: those earliest offers
—How can I forget?—EACH POEM GUARANTEED
A LIE OR PERMANENTLY IRRELEVANT.
WE FURNISH POEMS *AND* READERS. What a slogan!
(I had only to give credit to "my daemon";
Say, confidentially, "dictated by the devil.")
I can still see my picture in that schoolroom.
And next—who has it now?—*The World's Enormity,*

That novel of the Wandering Jewess, Lilith,
Who went to bed with six millennia.
(It came complete with sales, scenario,
And testimonials of grateful users:
Not like a book at all. . . . Beats life. . . .)

Beats life.

How ill we knew each other then! how mockingly
I nodded, "Almost thou persuadest me,"
And made my offer:

"If ever I don't say
To the hour of life that I can wish for: *Stay,*
Thou art so fair! why, you may have my—
Shadow."

Our real terms were different
And signed and sealed for good, neither in blood
Nor ink but in my life: *Neither to live*
Nor ask for life—that wasn't a bad bargain
For a poor devil of a poet, was it?
One makes a solitude and calls it peace.
So you phrased it; yet—yet—one is paid:
To see things as they are, to make them what they might be—
Old Father of Truths, old Spirit that Accepts—
That's something. . . . If, afterwards, we broke our bargain—

He interrupts: *But what nobility!*
I once saw a tenor at the Opéra Comique
Who played the Fisher—of Pearls or else of Souls.
He wore a leopard-skin, lay down, and died;
And sang ten minutes lying on his side
And died again; and then, applauded,
Gave six bows, leaning on his elbow,
And at the seventh started on his encore.
He was, I think, a poet.

Renounce, renounce,

You sing in your pure clear grave ardent tones
And then give up—whatever you're afraid to take,
Which is everything; and after that take credit
For dreaming something else to take its place.
Isn't what is already enough for you?
Must you always be making *something?*
Must each fool cook a lie up all his own?
You beings, won't even being disgust you
With causing something else to be? Make, make—
You squeak like mice; and yet it's all hypocrisy—
How often each of you, in his own heart,
Has wiped the world out, and thought afterwards:
No need to question, now: *"If others are, am I?"*
Still, I confess that I and my good Neighbor
Have always rather envied you existence.
Your simple conceits!—but both of us enjoy them:
"Dear God, make me Innocent or Wise,"
Each card in the card-catalogue keeps praying;
And dies, and the divine Librarian
Rebinds him—
rebinds? that's odd; but then, He's odd
And as a rule—
I'm lying: there's no rule at all.
The world divides into—believe me—facts.

I see the devil can quote Wittgenstein.
He's blacker than he's painted.
Old ink-blot,
What are you, after all? A parody.
You can be satisfied? then how can I?
If you accept, is not that to deny?
A Dog in a tub, who was the Morning Star!
To have come down in the universe so far
As here, and now, and *this*—and all to buy

One bored, stoop-shouldered, sagging-cheeked particular
Lest the eternal bonfire fail—
                                        ah Lucifer!

But at *blacker* an embarrassed smile
Wavers across his muzzle, he breaks in:
It's odd that you've never guessed: I'm through.
To tempt, sometimes, a bored anachronism
Like you into— but why should I say what?
To stretch out by the Fire and improvise:
This pleases me, now there's no need for me.
Even you must see I'm obsolescent.
A specialist in personal relations,
I valued each of you at his own worth.
You had your faults; but you were bad at heart.
I disliked each life, I assure you, for its own sake.
—But to deal indifferently in life and death;
To sell, wholesale, piecemeal, annihilation;
To—I will not go into particulars—
This beats me.
                    To men, now, *I should give advice?*
I'm vain, as you know; but not ridiculous.
Here in my inglenook, shy, idle, I conclude:
I never understood them: *as the consequence*
They end without me. . . .
                                        "Scratch a doctor
And find a patient," I always used to say.
Now that I've time, I've analyzed myself
And find that I am growing, or have grown—
Was always, perhaps, indifferent.
It takes a man to love or hate a man
Wholeheartedly. And how wholeheartedly
You act out All that is deserves to perish!
As if to take me at my word—an idle mot

That no one took less seriously than I.
It was so, *of course; and yet—and yet—*

I find that I've grown used to you. Hell gives us habits
To take the place of happiness, alas!
When I look foward, it is with a pang
That I think of saying, "My occupation's gone."

But twelve's striking: time to be in bed.

I think: He's a changed—all this has shaken him.
He was always delicate: a spirit of society,
A way to come to terms—
now, no more terms!
Those pleasant evenings of denunciation!
How gratefully, after five acts' rejection,
A last firm shake and quaver and statistic,
He'd end, *falsetto:* "But let's be realistic"—
Had he, perhaps, exaggerated? He had exaggerated . . .
How quietly, a little later, he'd conclude:
"I accept it all."
And now to be unable
To accept, to have exaggerated—
to do anything:
It's hard for him. How often he has said,
"I like you for always doing as you please"—
He couldn't. Free will appealed so much to him;
He thought, I think: *If they've the choice . . .*
He was right. And now, to have no choice!

CHILDREN

A Sick Child

The postman comes when I am still in bed.
"Postman, what do you have for me today?"
I say to him. (But really I'm in bed.)
Then he says—what shall I have him say?

"This letter says that you are president
Of —this word here; it's a republic."
Tell them I can't answer right away.
"It's your duty." No, I'd rather just be sick.

Then he tells me there are letters saying everything
That I can think of that I want for them to say.
I say, "Well, thank you very much. Good-bye."
He is ashamed, and turns and walks away.

If I can think of it, it isn't what I want.
I want . . . I want a ship from some near star
To land in the yard, and beings to come out
And think to me: "So this is where you are!

Come." Except that they won't do,
I thought of them. . . . And yet somewhere there must be
Something that's different from everything.
All that I've never thought of—think of me!

The Black Swan

When the swans turned my sister into a swan
I would go to the lake, at night, from milking:
The sun would look out through the reeds like a swan,
A swan's red beak; and the beak would open
And inside there was darkness, the stars and the moon.

Out on the lake a girl would laugh.
"Sister, here is your porridge, sister,"
I would call; and the reeds would whisper,
"Go to sleep, go to sleep, little swan."
My legs were all hard and webbed, and the silky

Hairs of my wings sank away like stars
In the ripples that ran in and out of the reeds:
I heard through the lap and hiss of water
Someone's "Sister . . . sister," far away on the shore,
And then as I opened my beak to answer

I heard my harsh laugh go out to the shore
And saw—saw at last, swimming up from the green
Low mounds of the lake, the white stone swans:
The white, named swans . . . "It is all a dream,"
I whispered, and reached from the down of the pallet

To the lap and hiss of the floor.
And "Sleep, little sister," the swans all sang
From the moon and stars and frogs of the floor.
But the swan my sister called, "Sleep at last, little sister,"
And stroked all night, with a black wing, my wings.

A Quilt-Pattern

The blocked-out Tree
Of the boy's Life is gray
On the tangled quilt: the long day
Dies at last, after many tales.
Good me, bad me, the Other
Black out, and the humming stare
Of the woman—the good mother—
Drifts away; the boy falls
Through darkness, the leagues of space
Into the oldest tale of all.

All the graves of the forest
Are opened, the scaling face
Of a woman—the dead mother—
Is square in the steam of a yard
Where the cages are warmed all night for the rabbits,
All small furry things
That are hurt, but that never cry at all—
That are skinned, but that never die at all.
Good me, bad me
Dry their tears, and gather patiently
Through the loops of the chicken-wire of the cages
Blackberries, the small hairy things
They live on, here in the wood of the dream.

Here a thousand stones
Of the trail home shine from their strings
Like just-brushed, just-lost teeth.
All the birds of the forest
Sit brooding, stuffed with crumbs.
But at home, far, far away

The white moon shines from the stones of the chimney,
His white cat eats up his white pigeon.

But the house hums, "We are home." Good me, bad me
Sits wrapped in his coat of rabbit-skin
And looks for some little living thing
To be kind to, for then it will help him—
There is nothing to help; good me
Sits twitching the rabbit's-fur of his ears
And says to himself, "My mother is basting
Bad me in the bath-tub—"
                                        the steam rises,
A washcloth is turned like a mop in his mouth.
He stares into the mouth
Of the whole house: there in it is waiting—
No, there is nothing.

He breaks a finger
From the window and lifts it to his—
"Who is nibbling at me?" says the house.
The dream says, "The wind,
The heaven-born wind";
The boy says, "It is a mouse."
He sucks at the finger; and the house of bread
Calls to him in its slow singing voice:
"Feed, feed! Are you fat now?
Hold out your finger."
The boy holds out the bone of the finger.
It moves, but the house says, "No, you don't know.
Eat a little longer."
The taste of the house
Is the taste of his—
                                "I don't know,"
Thinks the boy. "No, I don't *know!*"

His whole dream swells with the steam of the oven
Till it whispers, "You are full now, mouse—
Look, I have warmed the oven, kneaded the dough:
Creep in—ah, ah, it is warm!—
Quick, we can slip the bread in now," says the house.
He whispers, "I do not know
How I am to do it."
"Goose, goose," cries the house,
"It is big enough—just look!
See, if I bend a little, so—"

He has moved. . . . He is still now, and holds his breath.
If something is screaming itself to death
There in the oven, it is not the mouse
Nor anything of the mouse's. Bad me, good me
Stare into each other's eyes, and timidly
Smile at each other: it was the Other.

But they are waking, waking; the last stair creaks—
Out there on the other side of the door
The house creaks, "How is my little mouse? Awake?"
It is she.
He says to himself, "I will never wake."
He says to himself, not breathing:
"Go away. Go away. Go away."

And the footsteps go away.

Afterwards

(Four adaptations from Corbière's *Rondels pour après*)

I

Sleep: here's your bed . . . You'll not come, any more, to ours.
The hungry sleep, and are fed?—Your tongue is all grass.
Sleep: oh, they love you, now—the loved one is always
The Other. Dream: the last fields are all flowers.

Sleep: they'll call you star-snatcher, bareback-rider
Of the rays! . . . though it will be dark there, very dark.
And the angel of attics, at dusk—lean spider,
Hope—comes to spin, for your vacant brow, its webs.

Veiled silencer! . . . But for you a kiss is waiting
Under the veil . . . where, no one knows; close your eyes to see.
Laugh: here under the pall, the first prize is waiting.

—They'll break your nose with a smart blow of the censer,
A fine bouquet! for the big, blooming, tallowy mug
Of a well-to-do sexton with his candle-snuffer.

II

It's getting dark, little thief of starlight!
There're no nights any longer, there're no days.
Sleep . . . till they come for you, child, some morning—
Those who said: *Never!* Those who said: *Always!*

Do you hear their steps? They are not heavy:
Oh, the light feet!—Love has wings . . .
It's getting dark, little thief of starlight!

Don't you hear them asking? . . . You're not listening.
Sleep: it's light, your load of everlastings.
They're not coming at all, your friends the bears,
To throw bricks at your bottle of fireflies.
It's getting dark, little thief of starlight!

III

Good morning! . . . Go to sleep: your candle-end
Is there where they put it; then they left you.
You're not afraid of being alone, though—
Poor little thing, are you? It's light as day.

You scared of that old maid and her ruler!
Go on! . . . Why, who's got the nerve to wake you?
Good evening! . . . Go to sleep: your candle-end . . .

Is out.—There's not even a janitor:
Only, the north wind, the south wind, will come to weigh
In their great scales, a thread of gossamer.
—*They* drive you out in the cold, those flatfeet!
Good night! . . . Go to sleep: your candle-end . . .

IV

Run away, little comet's-hair-comber!
The wild grass, in the wind, will be your hair;
From your broken eye there will gush out the
Will-o'-the-wisps, prisoners in your weak head.

The grave-flowers they call Love-in-Idleness
Will seed there, to swell your earthy laugh . . .
And Solitary's flowers, forget-me-nots.

Go, little poet: your coffin's a plaything
For the undertaker's-men, a sound-box
For your penitentiary's last siren . . .
They think you're dead—they're so dumb, these grown-ups—
Run away, little comet's-hair-comber!

The Night Before the Night Before Christmas

(1934)

In the Arden Apartments
Only a community center and an apartment
From the new lots and the old forest
Of Hillsboro Manor
Lived a girl and her father,
Her aunt, and her one brother.
Nights, warm in her bed,
The girl would still dream of the mother
Who, two years dead,
Looks more like her sister than her mother
—So they had said—
And lays, slowly, a dark shining head
On the dark, stooped shoulder
Of the girl's new teacher.
Is there any question?
The girl has forgotten to answer
And watches him open the door of the cab
That is bringing an Invitation to the Dance:
Till Mother disappears in fur,
The girl trails toward the house
And stares at her bitten nails, her bare red knees—
And presses her chapped, cold hands together
In a middy blouse.

The night before the night before Christmas
Her brother looked out over the snow
That had fallen all day, and saw her

At last, two floors below,
And knocked at the window—drawn-over, frosted-over—
Till she waved and made an O
With her mouth—she was calling.
As she climbed the stairs the snow
Stopped falling, she saw from the landing
Past the big old houses, the small new houses,
And the wood's scrambled boughs
The sun in the hills. . . .
                                        Home, home.
She throws her books on the sofa,
And the boy, from his bed,
Calls to her: "Mother, what is snow?"
She answers: "It is the cotton-wool, my Son,
That is falling from the ears of God."
The boy says: "Ho ho ho!
But tell me, Mother,
Why does He keep it in His ears?"
She answers:
"My Son, that He may not hear
How hideously men use His name."

The boy calls, "No, *mis*use, *mis*use!"
She says, "It's just the same."
But she says to herself as she turns on the light in her room:
"How hideously men use His name. . . ."

And she and her father eat dinner with her aunt
And she carries a tray to her brother;
She can hear carols from the radio
In the living-room, as she looks for the dominoes.
After that she offers to read her brother
Another chapter from *The Iron Heel.*
"No, read me from *Stalky.*"

She starts to, but says, "When I was your age
I read it all the time." He answers, "It's not real."
She cries, "Oh *isn't* it! Why, in Germany—"
But she stops and finally says, "Well . . ."
And reads about Regulus leaving, full of courage,
For that nigger Manchester, Carthage.
She reads it, *that Negro Manchester,*
But it's just the same, he doesn't understand.
She laughs, and says to her brother:
"Engels lived in Manchester."
The boy says: "Who was Engels?"
She says: "Don't you even remember *that?"*

In her room that night she looks at herself in the mirror
And thinks: "Do I really look like *that?"*
She stares at her hair;
It's really a beautiful golden—anyway, yellow:
She brushes it with affection
And combs her bang back over so it slants.
How white her teeth are.
A turned-up nose . . .
No, it's no use.
She thinks: What do I *really* look like?
I don't know.

Not really.
Really.

Some dolls and a letter sweater
And a beige fur bear,
A Pink and a Golden and a Blue
Fairy Book, all, all in a row,
Beam from the light, bright, white-starred blue
Of the walls, the clouding curtains—

Anachronisms
East of the sun and west of the moon.
She wraps in white tissue paper
A shiny *Coming Struggle for Power*
For her best friend—
And ties it, one gold, gritty end
Of the string in her mouth, and one in her left hand;
Her right forefinger presses down the knot. . . .
She wraps some improving and delightful
Things she has got for her brother
And one medium-sized present for her aunt
And the gloves she has knitted, the tie she has picked
For her father—poor Lion,
Poor Moose.
She'd give him something that means something
But it's no use:
People are so *dumb*.
She thinks with regretful indignation:
"Why, he might as well not be alive . . ."
And sees all the mottoes at his office,
Like *Do It Now*
And *To Travel Hopefully*
Is A Better Thing Than To Arrive.

Still, he was sorry when my squirrel . . .
He was sorry as Brother when my squirrel . . .
When the gifts are wrapped she reads.

Outside, the wind is—whatever it is;
Inside, it is its own old
Terrible comfortable self:
A ghost in a story—it is all a story.
An uneasy, rocking, comfortable tune
Keeps singing itself under the cold words

In her warm head—cold world
In her warm head—
                                        in Praise of Learning:
  LEARN it, WOmen in KITCHens . . .
  LEARN it, MEN of SEVenty . . .
She goes on turning
The big small-printed pages—
A kind of world . . .
                                          Use-, surplus-, and exchange-
Value (all these, and plain
Value)
Creak slowly by, the wagon groans—
Creak by, like rags, like bottles—
Like rags, like bottles, like old bones . . .
The bones of men. Her breath is quickened
With pitying, indignant pain.
She thinks: *That's* funny . . .
That's funny: a *Cyclopean* machine . . .
It blinks at her with one blind eye.
Who put your eye out?
                                              No one.
Watching with parted lips,
A shy sidelong stare,
She makes out, far off, among columns
Of figures, the children laboring:
A figure buried among figures
Looks at her beggingly, a beast in pain.
She puts her hand
Out into the darkness till it touches:
Her flesh freezes, in that instant, to the iron
And pulls away in blood.
The tears of pain,
Of her own passive, guilty, useless pain
Swell in her eyes, she blinks them over and over

LEARN it, MEN of SEVen
By your mothers, in the mills—
WHAT you don't LEARN yourSELF you don't KNOW.

She thinks of her brother going down
To the pits with the ponies, too soon for the sun,
And coming back black, too late for the sun—
No school—he wouldn't even know
Who God is, like the one
In the book—
not even know
Enough not to believe in God . . .
She thinks, as she has thought,
Her worn old thought,
By now one word:
"But how could this world be
If he's all-powerful, all-good?
No—there's no God."

She reads.

The figures, the values, the one Value
Are clothed with the cloud of her breathing—
The voice echoing over
The dark, stooped shoulder
Ends, hissing a little: "is un*just*."
The hiss blurs in her head
With the hiss of her slow breath,
The lumps of her feet, her lashes
Stuck fast together, washed shut forever, on the wave
Of . . . that is washing, over and over, on the shore
Of . . . something . . . Something . . .
But her head jerks straight,
The song strengthens, its last words strike home:

YOU must be READy to take POWer!
YOU must be READy to take POWer!

She is reading a Factory Act, a girl in a room.

And afterwards—the room is getting colder
And she is too tired to hold her head up any longer—
She puts away her book
And gives her hair its counted-off
Strokes, and works in and wipes off
Some cold cream from her jar
Of Rexall's Theatrical Cold Cream; and puts on, yawning
Over and over, her boy's blue silk pajamas,
Her white birthday Angora
Bed-socks. She puts up the window—
Her radiator clanks a minute
As someone in the basement banks
The furnace for the night—
And she puts out the light.

She lies half-in, half-out of moonlight
In the sheer cold of the fresh
Sheets, under the patched star-pattern
Of the quilt; and, curled there, warms a world
Out slowly, a wobbling blind ellipse
That lengthens in half a dozen jumps
Of her numb shrinking feet,
Steadies . . . A train wails, over and over,
At a crossing. "It's like Martha,"
She mumbles. "So's the radiator."
The long, mourning, hollow questions
Of Martha Locomotive-Engineer
(You can't get more than a snore
From Martha Janitor, asleep by now

On his brass bed in the basement)
Vex Mary, in her bed-socks, listening guiltily
To the hollow answers of her Lord.
The poor, the poor . . .
                                        Her wandering mind
Comes to what was a joy,
What is a sorrow—
A cave opening into the dark
Earth, down to the dead:
What, played with day after day,
Stroked, called to, fed
In the small, wild, straggling park—
Told of, night after night, to the boy
Who listened, longing, among the games
Strewn on his rumpled bed—
                                        was gone, one winter day.
She thought: "Tomorrow
He will be where he always is"; and tomorrow
She thought: "He will be here again, tomorrow.
He is asleep with all the other squirrels
There in the hollow of his favorite tree.
He is living on all the nuts he hid
In his cave in the hollow tree."

On warm days, all that winter,
All the warm days of the spring,
She saw the others—never hers;
She thought, trying not to think, "Why, *anything*
Could have happened to him"; she thought, as the living
Think of their life, "Oh, it's not *right!*"
The squirrels are chattering
From leaf to leaf, as her squirrel chattered:
The Poor, the Poor . . .
They have eaten, rapidly,

From her hand, as though to say:
"But you won't hurt me, will you? *Will you?*"

They have nothing to lose but their lives.
She looks home into
The lancing eyes
In the rat-like face, the sucking
Fish-hooks of the little paws: a clawed
Rat with an Angora tail. A clawed
Dead rat with an Angora tail.

There is something deep
Under her will, against her will,
That keeps murmuring to her, "It's so";
And she murmurs, almost asleep:
"Un*just*—no, it's not *so*.
If he were educated . . ."
She sees six squirrels in a row
Thinking in chorus, in slow, low,
Hissing, radiator-steam-valve voices:
"Wherefore Art Thou, Romeo?"
The big squirrel says, "No.
No, that is not *just* it.
Try it again."
Their skein-silk lashes
Tremble, and they look sidelong up at her—
And cry, softly, in their sly,
Dumb, scared, malicious pain . . .
And try it again.

A dream, a dream.
She whispers: "I'm awake.
No, I'm not dreaming, I'm awake."

There is no more moonlight.
Out there, there is darkness and light,
The cold of night.
The world is no longer hidden
By the fire of her lit room,
By the day of the light of the sun.
Out there nothing moves except with a faint
Choked straining shiver;
Sounds except with a faint
Choked croaking sigh.
They are all there together.

Up over
The last twig, in the wild still sky,
Far under the last root, in the wild still sky,
There is another galaxy
Of so many hundreds of thousands of stars
So many hundreds of thousands of years
Away; and it is one
Of so many hundreds of thousands
Of galaxies—some like our own.
It is good, it is evil?
The girl gives her long straining sigh—
In the cells of the needles of the branches
Of the evergreens, the sap is ice.
Wherever the girl stares—
Hung out over, hung in under
The abyss that is her home—
There is something, something: the universe
Is a mirror backed with black
Out of which her face shines back
In the midst of hundreds of millions of suns.

They are all there together.

In the fields outside
There is not one step on the snow,
And each bough is bent with the burden
That is greater, almost, than it can bear.
The breaths of a world are webs
Of angelhair,
Of glass spun, life by life,
Into the trees' earned, magic tinsel.
A handful
Of snowflakes falls from a branch to a bush;
A star hovers
At the tip of a frozen spruce.
It disappears.
(At the side of the shepherds Hansel
Stands hand in hand with Gretel
And sparkles, under a sparkling star,
Like Lot's own wife:
Bushes, bushes.)
When the owl calls nothing answers.
In the owl's lungs, strained through feathers,
A breath is the edge of a knife. . . .
The haze of the girl's slow breaths,
Of her spun-sugar, cotton-candy breath,
Floats up, clouding the printed stars
Of the faint walls: white
As the down of the wing of an angel; white
As the beard of Friedrich Engels. . . .

In the fields there is not one angel.
In all these fields
There is not one thing that knows
It is almost Christmas.
                                        Staring, staring
At the gray squirrel dead in the snow,

She and her brother float up from the snow—
The last crumbs of their tears
Are caught by the birds that are falling
To strew their leaves on the snow
That is covering, that has covered
The play-mound under the snow. . . .
The leaves are the snow, the birds are the snow,
The boy and girl in the leaves of their grave
Are the wings of the bird of the snow.
But her wings are mixed in her head with the Way
That streams from their shoulders, stars like snow:
They spread, at last, their great starry wings
And her brother sings, "I am dying."

"No: it's not so, not so—
Not *really,"*
She thinks; but she says, "You are dying."
He says, "I didn't know."

And she cries: "I don't know, I don't know, I don't know!"

They are flying.

They look down over the earth.
There is not one crumb.
The rays of the stars of their wings
Strike the boughs of the wood, and the shadows
Are caught up into the night,
The first faint whisper of the wind:
Home, home, whispers the wind;
There are shadows of stars, a working
Hand in the . . .

There are words on the graves of the snow.
She whispers, "When I was alive,

I read them all the time.
I read them all the time."
And he whispers, sighing:
"When I was alive . . ."

And, moving her licked, chapped, parted lips,
She reads, from the white limbs' vanished leaves:
To End Hopefully
Is A Better Thing—
A Far, Far Better Thing—
It is a far, far better thing . . .

She feels, in her hand, her brother's hand.
She is crying.

ONCE UPON A TIME

A Girl in a Library

An object among dreams, you sit here with your shoes off
And curl your legs up under you; your eyes
Close for a moment, your face moves toward sleep . . .
You are very human.
                                        But my mind, gone out in tenderness,
Shrinks from its object with a thoughtful sigh.
This is a waist the spirit breaks its arm on.
The gods themselves, against you, struggle in vain.
This broad low strong-boned brow; these heavy eyes;
These calves, grown muscular with certainties;
This nose, three medium-sized pink strawberries
—But I exaggerate. In a little you will leave:
I'll hear, half squeal, half shriek, your laugh of greeting—
Then, *decrescendo,* bars of that strange speech
In which each sound sets out to seek each other,
Murders its own father, marries its own mother,
And ends as one grand transcendental vowel.

(Yet for all I know, the Egyptian Helen spoke so.)
As I look, the world contracts around you:
I see Brünnhilde had brown braids and glasses
She used for studying; Salome straight brown bangs,
A calf's brown eyes, and sturdy light-brown limbs

Dusted with cinnamon, an apple-dumpling's . . .
Many a beast has gnawn a leg off and got free,
Many a dolphin curved up from Necessity—
The trap has closed about you, and you sleep.
If someone questioned you, *What doest thou here?*
You'd knit your brows like an orangoutang
(But not so sadly; not so thoughtfully)
And answer with a pure heart, guilelessly:
I'm studying. . . .
                    If only you were not!
Assignments,
            recipes,
                    the *Official Rulebook*
Of Basketball—ah, let them go; you needn't mind.
The soul has no assignments, neither cooks
Nor referees: it wastes its time.
                              It wastes its time.
Here in this enclave there are centuries
For you to waste: the short and narrow stream
Of Life meanders into a thousand valleys
Of all that was, or might have been, or is to be.
The books, just leafed through, whisper endlessly . . .
Yet it is hard. One sees in your blurred eyes
The "uneasy half-soul" Kipling saw in dogs'.
One sees it, in the glass, in one's own eyes.
In rooms alone, in galleries, in libraries,
In tears, in searchings of the heart, in staggering joys
We memorize once more our old creation,
Humanity: with what yawns the unwilling
Flesh puts on its spirit, O my sister!

So many dreams! And not one troubles
Your sleep of life? no self stares shadowily
From these worn hexahedrons, beckoning

With false smiles, tears? . . .
Meanwhile Tatyana
Larina (gray eyes nickel with the moonlight
That falls through the willows onto Lensky's tomb;
Now young and shy, now old and cold and sure)
Asks, smiling: "But what is she dreaming of, fat thing?"
I answer: She's not fat. She isn't dreaming.
She purrs or laps or runs, all in her sleep;
Believes, awake, that she is beautiful;
She never dreams.
Those sunrise-colored clouds
Around man's head—that inconceivable enchantment
From which, at sunset, we come back to life
To find our graves dug, families dead, selves dying:
Of all this, Tanya, she is innocent.
For nineteen years she's faced reality:
They look alike already.
They say, man wouldn't be
The best thing in this world—and isn't he?—
If he were not too good for it. But she
—She's good enough for it.
And yet sometimes
Her sturdy form, in its pink strapless formal,
Is as if bathed in moonlight—modulated
Into a form of joy, a Lydian mode;
This Wooden Mean's a kind, furred animal
That speaks, in the Wild of things, delighting riddles
To the soul that listens, trusting . . .
Poor senseless Life:
When, in the last light sleep of dawn, the messenger
Comes with his message, you will not awake.
He'll give his feathery whistle, shake you hard,
You'll look with wide eyes at the dewy yard
And dream, with calm slow factuality:

"Today's Commencement. My bachelor's degree
In Home Ec., my doctorate of philosophy
In Phys. Ed.
                    [Tanya, they won't even *scan*]
Are waiting for me. . . ."
                                        Oh, Tatyana,
The Angel comes: better to squawk like a chicken
Than to say with truth, "But I'm a *good* girl,"
And Meet his Challenge with a last firm strange
Uncomprehending smile; and—then, then!—see
The blind date that has stood you up: your life.
(For all this, if it isn't, perhaps, life,
Has yet, at least, a language of its own
Different from the books'; worse than the books'.)
And yet, the ways we miss our lives are life.
Yet . . . yet . . .
                    to have one's life add up to *yet!*

You sigh a shuddering sigh. Tatyana murmurs,
"Don't cry, little peasant"; leaves us with a swift
"Good-bye, good-bye . . . Ah, don't think ill of me . . ."
Your eyes open: you sit here thoughtlessly.

I love you—and yet—and yet—I love you.

Don't cry, little peasant. Sit and dream.
One comes, a finger's width beneath your skin,
To the braided maidens singing as they spin;
There sound the shepherd's pipe, the watchman's rattle
Across the short dark distance of the years.
I am a thought of yours: and yet, you do not think . . .
The firelight of a long, blind, dreaming story
Lingers upon your lips; and I have seen
Firm, fixed forever in your closing eyes,
The Corn King beckoning to his Spring Queen.

The Sleeping Beauty: Variation of the Prince

After the thorns I came to the first page.
He lay there gray in his fur of dust:
As I bent to open an eye, I sneezed.
But the ball looked by me, blue
As the sky it stared into . . .
And the sentry's cuirass is red with rust.

Children play inside: the dirty hand
Of the little mother, an inch from the child
That has worn out, burst, and blown away,
Uncurling to it—does not uncurl.
The bloom on the nap of their world
Is set with thousands of dawns of dew.

But at last, at the center of all the webs
Of the realm established in your blood,
I find you; and—look!—the drop of blood
Is there still, under the dust of your finger:
I force it, slowly, down from your finger
And it falls and rolls away, as it should.

And I bend to touch (just under the dust
That was roses once) the steady lips
Parted between a breath and a breath
In love, for the kiss of the hunter, Death.
Then I stretch myself beside you, lay
Between us, there in the dust, His sword.

When the world ends—it will never end—
The dust at last will fall from your eyes

In judgment, and I shall whisper:
"For hundreds of thousands of years I have slept
Beside you, here in the last long world
That you had found; that I have kept."

When they come for us—no one will ever come—
I shall stir from my long light sleep,
I shall whisper, "Wait, wait! . . . She is asleep."
I shall whisper, gazing, up to the gaze of the hunter,
Death, and close with the tips of the dust of my hand
The lids of the steady—
                    Look, He is fast asleep!

La Belle au Bois Dormant

She lies, her head beneath her knees,
In their old trunk; and no one comes—
No porter, even, with a check
Or forceps for her hard delivery.
The trains pant outside; and she coils breathlessly
Inside his wish and is not waked.

She is sleeping but, alas! not beautiful.
Travelers doze around; are borne away;
And the thorns clamber up her stony veins.
She is irreparable; and yet a state
Asks for her absently, and citizens
Drown for an instant in her papery eyes.

Yet where is the hunter black enough to storm
Her opening limbs, or shudder like a fish
Into the severed maelstrom of her skull?
The blood fondles her outrageous mouth;
The lives flourish in her life, to alienate
Their provinces from her outranging smile.

What wish, what keen pain has enchanted her
To this cold period, the end of pain,
Wishes, enchantment: this suspending sleep?
She waits here to be waked—as he has waited
For her to wake, for her to wake—
Her lips set in their slack conclusive smile.

The Island

"While sun and sea—and I, and I—
Were warped through summer on our spar,
I guessed beside the fin, the gull,
And Europe ebbing like a sail
A life indifferent as a star.

"My lids were grating to their close,
My palms were loosening to die,
When—failing through its drift of surf,
Whale-humped, its beaches cracked with salt—
The island gave its absent sigh.

"Years notched my hut, my whiskers soughed
Through summer's witless stare: blue day
Flickered above the nothingness
That rimmed me, the unguessed abyss
Broke on my beaches, and its spray

"Frosted or salted with its curling smile
The printless hachures of the sand . . .
I lay with you, Europe, in a net of snows:
And all my trolls—their noses flattened into Lapps'
Against the thin horn of my windows—wept;

"Vole, kobold, the snowshoe-footed hare
—Crowned with the smoke of steamboats, shagg'd with stars—
Whispered to my white mistress: *He is Mars;*
Till I called, laughing: *Friends! subjects! customers!*
And her face was a woman's, theirs were men's.

"All this I dreamed in my great ragged bed . . .
Or so I dreamed. The dawn's outspeaking smile

Curled through my lashes, felled the Märchen's wood;
The sun stripped my last cumulus of stars,
And the sea graved all the marshes of the swan.

"So, so. The years ticked past like crabs
Or an hour inched out to heaven, like the sea.
One day, by my black hand, my beard
Shone silver; I looked in astonishment
And pinched my lean calves, drawn with many scars,

"With my stiff fingers, till the parrot called
In my grum, quavering voice: *Poor Robinson!*
My herd came bleating, licked my salty cheeks;
I sobbed, and petted with a kind of love
These joys of mine—the old, half-human loves

"That had comforted my absent life . . .
I have dreamed of men, and I am old.
There is no Europe." The man, the goats, the parrot
Wait in their grove for death; and there floods to them
In its last thundering spray, the sea, the sea!

Hope

The spirit killeth, but
the letter giveth life.

The week is dealt out like a hand
That children pick up card by card.
One keeps getting the same hand.
One keeps getting the same card.

But twice a day—except on Saturday—
But every day—except on Sunday—
The wheel stops, there is a crack in Time:
With a hiss of soles, a rattle of tin,
My own gray Daemon pauses on the stair,
My own bald Fortune lifts me by the hair.

Woe's me! woe's me! In Folly's mailbox
Still laughs the postcard, Hope:
Your uncle in Australia
Has died and you are Pope.
For many a soul has entertained
A Mailman unawares—
And as you cry, Impossible,
A step is on the stairs.

One keeps getting the same dream
Delayed, marked *Postage Due,*
The bill that one has paid
Delayed, marked *Payment Due*—

Twice a day, in a rotting mailbox,
The white grubs are new:
And Faith, once more, is mine

Faithfully, but Charity
Writes hopefully about a new
Asylum—but Hope is as good as new.

Woe's me! woe's me! In Folly's mailbox
Still laughs the postcard, Hope:
Your uncle in Australia
Has died and you are Pope.
For many a soul has entertained
A Mailman unawares—
And as you cry, Impossible,
A step is on the stairs.

Good-bye, Wendover; Good-bye, Mountain Home

(Wendover, Mountain Home, Lowrie, Kearns, Laredo: Second Air Force fields. Men going to Overseas Replacement Depots like Kearns were called ORD's.)

Wives on day-coaches traveling with a baby
From one room outside Lowrie to a room near Kearns.
Husbands firing into sagebrush near Wendover,
Mesquite outside Laredo: you're on Shipping. Kearns.

Or if it isn't Kearns, it might as well be Kearns.
(I asked the first sergeant up at Operations.
The Wac at Transportation says you're ORD.)
The orders are cut. I tell you you're on Shipping
And you might as well get used to it, you ORD's.

Wives on day-coaches crying, talking to sailors,
Going home, going somewhere from a room near Kearns.
Husbands getting shots for cholera, yellow fever,
And shipping in the morning on a train from Kearns.

Or if it wasn't Kearns, it might as well be Kearns.
(I asked, but they've forgotten. Up at History
There're no wives, no day-coaches, and no ORD.)
The book is finished. I tell you you're not in it
And you might as well get used to it, you ORD's.

Transient Barracks

(1944)

Summer. Sunset. Someone is playing
The ocarina in the latrine:
You Are My Sunshine. A man shaving
Sees—past the day-room, past the night K.P.'s
Bent over a G.I. can of beets
In the yard of the mess—the red and green
Lights of a runway full of '24's.
The first night flight goes over with a roar
And disappears, a star, among mountains.

The day-room radio, switched on next door,
Says, "The thing about you is, you're *real*."
The man sees his own face, black against lather,
In the steamed, starred mirror: it is real.
And the others—the boy in underwear
Hunting for something in his barracks-bags
With a money-belt around his middle—
The voice from the doorway: "Where's the C.Q.?"
"Who wants to know?" "He's gone to the movies."
"Tell him Red wants him to sign his clearance"—
These are. Are what? Are.

"Jesus Christ, what a field!"

A gunner without a pass keeps saying
To a gunner without a pass. The man
Puts down his razor, leans to the window,
And looks out into the pattern of the field,
Of light and of darkness. His throat tightens,
His lips stretch into a blinded smile.

He thinks, *The times I've dreamed that I was back . . .*
The hairs on the back of his neck stand up straight.

He only yawns, and finishes shaving.
When the gunner asks him, "When you leaving?"
He says: "I just got in. This is my field."
And thinks: *I'm back for good. The States, the States!*
He puts out his hand to touch it—
And the thing about it is, it's *real.*

Terms

I

One-armed, one-legged, and one-headed,
The pensioner sits in the sun.
He is telling a story to the leaf
Of the new maple in his new yard:
"The Department of the Interior has sent Jack Frost with a spray-gun
To paint you red."
The leaf pulls hard
To get away—it believes the man—
And a blue Chevrolet sedan
Draws up and leaves a check for the man in the mail-box.

"You're as good as dead,"
Says the man, with a mocking smile, to the leaf;
And somebody knocks
At the front door, the man doesn't answer,
But sits back in his white board chair—
Holding a mallet, by a stake with rainbow rings—
And rubs his eyes, and yawns like a dog when the dog
Next door whines and rattles its chain.
He looks at the leaf, as he looks at things,
With mixed feelings—
And says, "I've changed."

The good dreams keep haunting
The ghost with a check in the mail-box, the fox
With four quick brown wooden legs.
With one military brush, in the morning,
He pulls forward, or brushes back, the fair

Hair on the living head,
And brushes his firm white teeth, and the porcelain jacket
On his left front tooth, that is dead.
The leaf is alive, and it is going to be dead;
It is like any other leaf.
You keep flipping the coin and it comes down heads
And nobody has ever seen it come down anything but heads
And the man has stopped looking:
                                                            it's heads.

He looks at the leaf—it is green—
And says with a flat black leather gesture:
"Never again."

II

He says: "My arm and leg—
My wooden arm, my wooden leg—
Wrestled with each other all last night
The way you whet a carving-knife
Till they stood crisscross against dawn
Over what seemed to me a tomb.
I felt for the dog-tags on the cross.

"I could find one number on the leg
And a different number on the arm.
The grave was empty.

"I thought first, 'I have arisen,'
And looked up past the cross into the dawn
And saw my own head, burning there,
Go out.
          But in the darkness
The leaves fell one by one, like checks,

Into the grave;
And I thought: I am my own grave.

"Then I awoke: I could see the toaster
On its rack over the waffle-iron
And the dew on the wickets; at breakfast the bread
Pops up, all brown, from its—
'It's all a dream,'
I said to myself. 'I am a grave dreaming
That it is a living man.' "

The man, as he has learned to,
Gets up and walks to the door.
As he opens the door
He watches his hand opening the door
And holds out his good hand—
And stares at them both, and laughs;
Then he says softly: "I am a man."

Jonah

As I lie here in the sun
And gaze out, a day's journey, over Nineveh,
The sailors in the dark hold cry to me:
"What meanest thou, O sleeper? Arise and call upon
Thy God; pray with us, that we perish not."

All thy billows and thy waves passed over me.
The waters compassed me, the weeds were wrapped about my head;
The earth with her bars was about me forever.
A naked worm, a man no longer,
I writhed beneath the dead:

But thou art merciful.
When my soul was dead within me I remembered thee,
From the depths I cried to thee. For thou art merciful:
Thou hast brought my life up from corruption,
O Lord my God. . . . When the king said, "Who can tell

But God may yet repent, and turn away
From his fierce anger, that we perish not?"
My heart fell; for I knew thy grace of old—
In my own country, Lord, did I not say
That thou art merciful?

Now take, Lord, I beseech thee,
My life from me; it is better that I die . . .
But I hear, "Doest thou well, then, to be angry?"
And I say nothing, and look bitterly
Across the city; a young gourd grows over me

And shades me—and I slumber, clean of grief.
I was glad of the gourd. But God prepared
A worm that gnawed the gourd; but God prepared
The east wind, the sun beat upon my head
Till I cried, "Let me die!" And God said, "Doest thou well

To be angry for the gourd?"
And I said in my anger, "I do well
To be angry, even unto death." But the Lord God
Said to me, "Thou hast had pity on the gourd"—
And I wept, to hear its dead leaves rattle—

"Which came up in a night, and perished in a night.
And should I not spare Nineveh, that city
Wherein are more than six-score thousand persons
Who cannot tell their left hand from their right;
And also much cattle?"

The Venetian Blind

It is the first day of the world
Man wakes into: the bars of the blind
And their key-signature, a leaf,
Stream darkly to two warmths;
One trembles, becomes his face.
He floats from the sunlight
Into a shadowed place:
There is a chatter, a blur of wings—
But where is the edge of things?
Where does the world begin?
His dreams
Have changed into this day, this dream;
He thinks, "But where am I?"
A voice calls patiently:
"Remember."
He thinks, "But where am I?"
His great limbs are curled
Through sunlight, about space.
What is that, *remember?*
He thinks that he is younger
Than anything has ever been.
He thinks that he is the world.

But his soul and his body
Call, as the bird calls, their one word—
And he remembers.

He is lost in himself forever.

And the Angel he makes from the sunlight
Says in mocking tenderness:

"Poor stateless one, wert thou the world?"
His soul and his body
Say, "What hast thou made of us, thy servants?
We are sick. We are dull. We are old."
"Who is this man? We know him not," says the world.

They have spoken as he would have made them speak;
And who else is there to speak?

The bars of the sunlight fall to his face.

And yet something calls, as it has called:
"But where am *I*? But where am *I*?"

Seele im Raum

It sat between my husband and my children.
A place was set for it—a plate of greens.
It had been there: I had seen it
But not somehow—but this was like a dream—
Not seen it so that I knew I saw it.
It was as if I could not know I saw it
Because I had never once in all my life
Not seen it. It was an eland.
An eland! *That* is why the children
Would ask my husband, for a joke, at Christmas:
"Father, is it Donner?" He would say, "No, Blitzen."
It had been there always. Now we put silver
At its place at meals, fed it the same food
We ourselves ate, and said nothing. Many times
When it breathed heavily (when it had tried
A long useless time to speak) and reached to me
So that I touched it—of a different size
And order of being, like the live hard side
Of a horse's neck when you pat the horse—
And looked with its great melting tearless eyes
Fringed with a few coarse wire-like lashes
Into my eyes, and whispered to me
So that my eyes turned backward in their sockets

And they said nothing—
                                        many times
I have known, when they said nothing,
That it did not exist. If they had heard
They *could* not have been silent. And yet they heard;
Heard many times what I have spoken

When it could no longer speak, but only breathe—
When I could no longer speak, but only breathe.

And, after some years, the others came
And took it from me—it was ill, they told me—
And cured it, they wrote me: my whole city
Sent me cards like lilac-branches, mourning
As I had mourned—
                    and I was standing
By a grave in flowers, by dyed rolls of turf,
And a canvas marquee the last brown of earth.

It is over.
It is over so long that I begin to think
That it did not exist, that I have never—
And my son says, one morning, from the paper:
"An eland. Look, an eland!"
                              —It was so.

Today, in a German dictionary, I saw *elend*
And the heart in my breast turned over, it was—

It was a word one translates *wretched*.

It is as if someone remembered saying:
"This is an antimacassar that I grew from seed,"
And this were true.
                    And, truly,
One could not wish for anything more strange—
For anything more. And yet it wasn't *interesting* . . .
—It was worse than impossible, it was a joke.

And yet when it was, I *was*—
Even to think that I once thought

That I could see it is to feel the sweat
Like needles at my hair-roots, I am blind

—It was not even a joke, not even a joke.

Yet how can I believe it? Or believe that I
Owned it, a husband, children? Is my voice the voice
Of that skin of being—of what owns, is owned
In honor or dishonor, that is borne and bears—
Or of that raw thing, the being inside it
That has neither a wife, a husband, nor a child
But goes at last as naked from this world
As it was born into it—

And the eland comes and grazes on its grave.

                                                This is senseless?
Shall I make sense or shall I tell the truth?
Choose either—I cannot do both.

I tell myself that. And yet it is not so,
And what I say afterwards will not be so:
To be at all is to be wrong.
                                                Being is being old
And saying, almost comfortably, across a table
From—
        from what I don't know—
                                                        in a voice
Rich with a kind of longing satisfaction:
"To own an eland! That's what I call life!"